Game of Thrones

Theme from the HBO Series

Music by Ramin Djawadi
Arranged for harp by Sylvia Woods

Performance Notes

This publication includes 2 harp arrangements of the theme from the HBO Series *"Game of Thrones"*.
The first arrangement requires a harp with 2 octaves below middle C.
The second arrangement is for smaller harps with 1 octave below middle C.

Thanks

I'd like to thank the following harpists for their help:
Paul Baker, Denise Grupp-Verbon, Allison Hampton, Rayven Hockett, and Anne Roos.

Game of Thrones
Theme from the HBO Series

This arrangement is for harps with 2 octaves below middle C.

Music by Ramin Djawadi
Arranged for harp by Sylvia Woods

If you do not have G sharping levers, or you want to omit the lever changes, you can delete measures 5 through 8. Please note that the right hand is written in the bass clef from in measures 10 through 24.

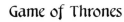

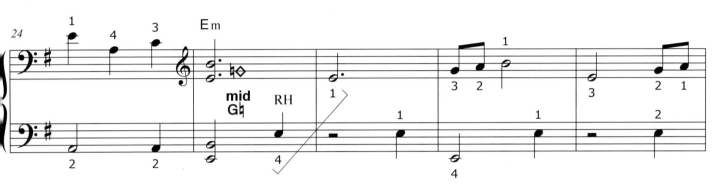

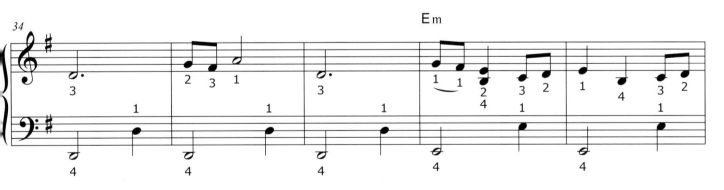

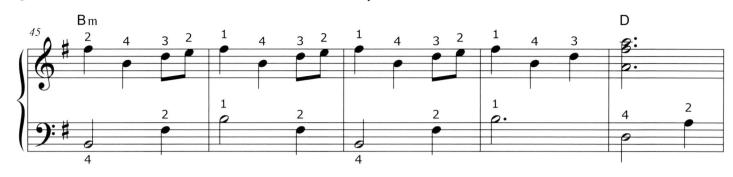

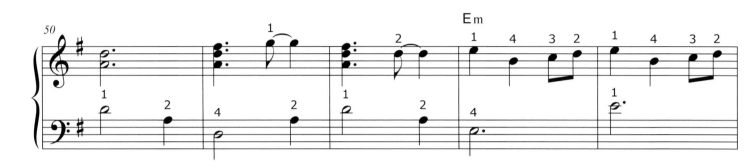

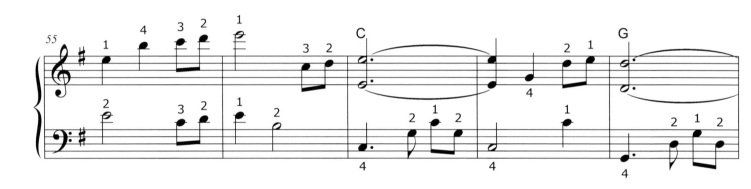

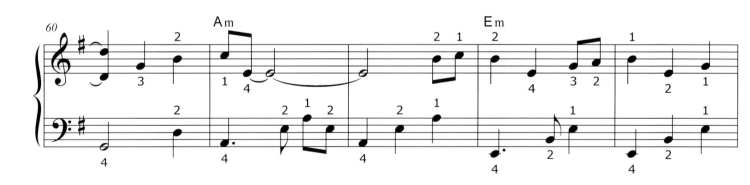

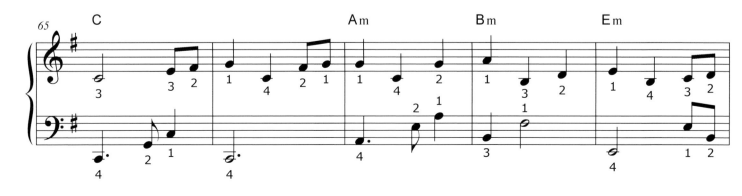

Game of Thrones
Theme from the HBO Series

Music by Ramin Djawadi
Arranged for harp by Sylvia Woods

This arrangement is for small harps with 1 octave below middle C.

If you do not have G sharping levers, or you want to omit the lever changes, you can delete measures 5 through 8.

Moderately fast

Game of Thrones

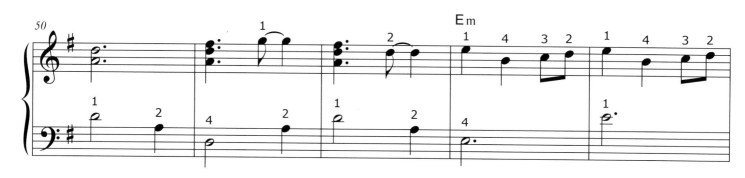

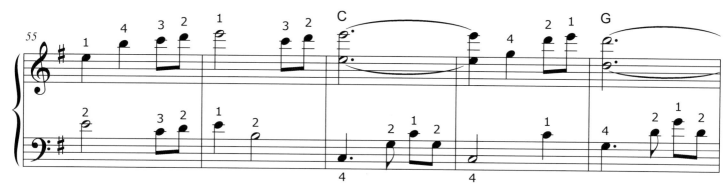

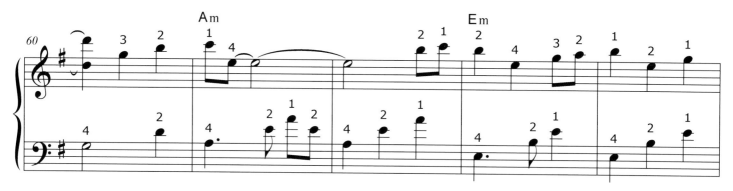

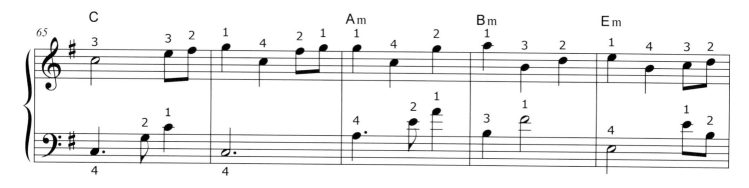